ANSEL
ADAMS

RICHARD WRIGLEY

SMITHMARK

This edition published in 1992
by SMITHMARK Publishers Inc.,
16 East 32nd Street,
New York, New York 10016

SMITHMARK books are available for
bulk purchase for sales promotion and
premium use. For details write or
telephone the Manager of Special
Sales, SMITHMARK Publishers Inc.,
16 East 32nd Street, New York, NY
10016. (212) 532-6600.

Produced by Brompton Books Corp.
15 Sherwood Place
Greenwich, CT 06830

ISBN 0-8317-0518-3

Printed in Hong Kong

10 9 8 7 6 5 4 3 2 1

LIST OF PLATES

INTRODUCTION

Ansel Adams' photographs, particularly those of landscape subjects, have come to be revered as timeless testimonials to the transcendent beauties of American nature. Adams himself encouraged this rhetoric, writing in 1974: 'Expression without doctrine, my photographs are . . . ends in themselves, images of the endless moments of the world.' The radiant intensity of Adams' photographs has been poignantly accentuated for late twentieth-century viewers, faced with a rapidly deteriorating environment and nostalgic for an unpolluted natural universe. Adams' images are celebrated not merely as evidence of the achievements of photographic art, but as austere icons of a lost, mythic domain. Adams himself has been turned into a persona at once saintly and simple in his dedication to photography and nature. Habitually portrayed in the literature on him as clad in boots, denim and stetson, he comes across as something between a Franciscan itinerant and a benevolent cowboy, rising before dawn to catch the morning light, then, fortified by rare steak and chips, setting out in search of the elusive photographic prey. However seductive such a perspective may be within which to admire Adams' work, it ignores the historically specific conditions which shaped his iconography and his photographic project. In order to understand this, we must consider his place within the context of early twentieth-century American photography.

Ansel Adams was born in San Francisco on February 20th 1902. He originally trained to be a concert pianist, and it was not until 1927 that he elected to pursue a career as a photographer. His early exploration of photography arose as a result of his employment in 1919 as custodian of the LeConte Memorial Lodge, the Sierra Club's headquarters in Yosemite Valley. The Sierra Club was made up of enthusiasts dedicated to the preservation of the majestic landscape of the Sierra Nevada. Adams' first published photographs appeared in the *Sierra Club Bulletin* from 1922 onward. Throughout his career, he was to be equally dedicated to the campaign to preserve the Sierra and the pursuit of photography – to a significant degree, these two activities were synonymous. Although he travelled widely in America, his prime subject remained the sublime landmarks and spaces of the Sierra. His first portfolio, published in 1927, was *Parmelian Prints of the High Sierra*. In 1928, he became the official photographer of the Sierra Club.

On a trip to Taos, New Mexico, in 1929, Adams met Alfred Stieglitz, Georgia

O'Keeffe, John Marin, and later Paul Strand. This encounter with some of the leading figures in modern American art and photography was inspirational. They responded enthusiastically to Adams' photographs, and Stieglitz, in particular, was to remain a kind of aesthetic guru for Adams. Stieglitz had gained a reputation as the highest champion of true art, and in particular as the guiding light in the creation of an authentic, indigenous American form of modern art, both through his own photographic practice and by furthering the careers of those whom he deemed to be kindred spirits. Adams never lost a self-deprecating reverence for Stieglitz and his work and regarded him as a supreme arbiter of what was worthy of admiration, despite the fact that they later differed on the probity of the New York Museum of Modern Art's promotion of photography. Whatever the sordid realities of Stieglitz's involvement with the art market, he projected himself as an intransigent proselytizer for modern American art. In a sense, Adams' trekking across mountainous terrain and his ascetic pursuit of pristine photographic motifs can be seen as analogous to Stieglitz's single-minded cult of the aesthetic. Adams, however, found sustenance in the natural wilderness, as against Stieglitz's fabrication of ethereal urban views; when Stieglitz looked to landscape, it was as a means to create oblique, fragmentary images that dematerialized their subject.

If Stieglitz made of photography a precious and ineffable art form, O'Keeffe's paintings of landscape and natural forms were infused by an organic, sensuous intensity. Marin's watercolours also evoked the power of landscape, but translated into an abbreviated, atmospheric idiom. In Paul Strand's photographs, Adams found a salutary antidote to what he referred to as the 'blurred, indefinite "poetic" prints' of Pictorialism. Pictorialism was a mode of photography which aspired to raise its status to that of art by mimicking the habits of composition and the artistic effects found in paintings. Strand, and Adams, rejected this in favour of immaculately crisp images deriving their resonance from their arresting detail and severity of content.

1932 was the year of Adams' first major one-man show, held at the De Young Memorial Museum in San Francisco. It was also the year when, together with other photographers such as Edward Weston, Imogen Cunningham and Willard Van Dyke, Adams formed the Group f 64. Amongst others, Dorothea Lange was later to join. The group's name referred to the use of a very small aperture which created photographs of great clarity and spacious depth of field. They deliberately produced no manifesto for they saw themselves as engaged in making what was ingenuously called 'straight photography', for which the best argument would be their photographs. This was intended to signal a contrast with the artificiality of Pictorialism. The relative informality of the group, however, meant that it only lasted until 1935.

The initiative to pursue a form of purist photography represented by the formation of the Group f 64 has to be seen in the context of the range of subjects and uses to which photography was being put in 1930s America, and in relation to earlier practices. If Stieglitz represented one extreme of photography, dedicated to realizing photographs as autonomous aesthetic objects, at the other pole was a large and diverse group of photographers committed to documenting contemporary life, for whom photography was a powerful but instrumental medium.

The greater part of early American photography had been involved with documentary, whether in the genre of portraiture, topography or scientific matters. By the early twentieth century, photography as a miraculously objective mode of recording gave way to more partial exploitations of its visual truthfulness. For example, Lewis Hine and Jacob A Riis had pioneered the photographic investigation of urban life. Hine was a sociologist and reformer, Riis a New York crime reporter. Riis surveyed slums and low-life milieux in order to demonstrate the need for housing reform, and thus to defuse the potentially disruptive unrest that such conditions might engender, whereas Hine looked into child labor and immigrant life with a far more sympathetic involvement. The photograph as visual document was put to full use by the Farm Security Administration in the 1930s and 1940s, initially as a means to call attention to chronic rural poverty during the Depression, and later to promote a more positive image of resilient, 'salt-of-the-earth' farming communities.

In a sense, Adams' work draws on both sides of these contrasting photographic rationales: on the one hand, the aestheticism exemplified by Stieglitz, on the other, early forms of partisan photojournalism. While Adams' commitment to producing uncompromisingly pure photographs was absolute, his purpose was consciously reformatory. His photographs of Yosemite were both a celebration of the incomparable beauties of this essentially American landscape, and a polemical evocation of something precious which was vulnerable to loss and deterioration unless it was securely protected from the depredations of modern life.

Adams self-consciously positioned himself in relation to these alternative practices. In a letter written in 1938 to Edward Weston, another exponent of 'straight photography', Adams reacted unequivocally to the book *Walker Evans: American Photographs*, which he saw as degrading the medium of photography:

Walker Evans' book gave me a hernia. I am so *goddam* mad over what people think America is from the left tier. Stinks, social and otherwise, are a poor exuse and imitation of the real beauty and power of the land and of the people inhabiting it. Evans has some beautiful things but they are lost in the shuffle of social significance.

Adams' anxiety over the representation of the land of America – at once a national concept and a topographical reality - is highly instructive insofar as it is symptomatic of his own line of thinking on this issue. While he was not unconcerned by social problems, he sought to resolve them by reference to the uncontaminated realm of nature. His landscape photographs encapsulate a puritan mode of pastoral. Contingent problems of the human condition are elided, and dwarfed, by the humbling majesty of towering mountains and vast panoramas of cloud and rock. In God's country, all men were equal. As he wrote to David McAlpin at the same time:

If I feel I have any niche at all in the photographic presentation of America, I think it would be chiefly to show the land and sky as the settings for human activity. And it would be showing also how man could be related to this magnificent setting, and how foolish it is that we have the disorganization and misery that we have.

It is interesting to note that Adams later warmed to Riis's safely distanced representations of poverty, more as amazingly faithful photographs, admirable for their simple but effective technique, than as disturbing social documents. In 1974, he wrote in the introduction to *Jacob A Riis: Photographer and Citizen*:

These people live again in print as intensely as when theur images were captured in the old dry plates of sixty years ago. . . . I am walking in their alleys, standing in their rooms and sheds and workshops, looking in an out of their windows. And they in turn seem to be aware of me.

1933 saw Adams heading east, to develop his acquaintance with leading photographers such as Stieglitz, Paul Strand, Charles Sheeler, and Edward Steichen. Adams sought recognition for his own work and also hoped to assess the state of the contemporary scene. In 1936 he had a well-received exhibition at 'An American Place', Stieglitz's gallery in New York. He also spent time in Washington in order to campaign for the interests of Yosemite National Park. In the same year he attended a conference in Washington on the national and state parks, where he was as active in badgering members of Congress to support conservation as he was back in California leading trips across the park, and, of course, taking photographs. A portfolio such as *Sierra Nevada: the John Muir Trail* (1938) was not merely a photo-essay, but also a polemical statement intended to inspire support for the preservation of the territory. His photographs were a homage by means of which he aimed to inspire a shared desire to value and protect the land. In the foreword, he set out his aim as ' the emotional interpretation of the Sierra Nevada' and:

The revelation of the beauty of wide horizons and the tender perfection of detail. No attempt is made to portray the Range in the manner of a catalogue. A detail of a tree root, a segment of a rock, a great paean of thunder clouds – all these relate with equal intensity to the portrayal of an impressive peak or canyon. The majesty of form, the solidity of stone, the eternal qualities of the Sierra as a noble gesture of the earth, cannot be transcribed in any but the richest and the most intense expression. Nevertheless, a certain objectivity must be maintained, a certain quality of reality adhered to, for these images – integrated through the camera – represent the most enduring and massive aspects of the world, and justify more than an abstract and esoteric interpretation. I feel secure in adhering to a certain austerity throughout, in accentuating the acuteness of edge and texture, and in stylizing the severity, grandeur, and poignant minutiae of the mountains.

In his foreword to *Portfolio III* (1960), a collection of prints spanning the period from

1926 to 1956, Adams reflected on his preoccupation with Yosemite and its meaning for him, both as a site for autobiographical musing, and also as a panacea for the tribulations of the modern world:

Yosemite Valley, to me, is always a sunrise, a glitter of green and golden wonder in a vast edifice of stone and space . . . After the initial excitement we begin to sense the need to share the living realities of this miraculous place. We may resent the intrusion of urban superficialities. We may be filled with regret that so much has happened to despoil, but we can also respond to the challenge to re-create, to protect, to re-interpret the enduring essence of Yosemite, to re-establish it as a sanctuary from the turmoil of time.

In 1940, Adams assisted Beaumont Newhall and David McAlpin in forming the Department of Photography at the Museum of Modern Art, New York. This institution was to play a key role in promoting not merely modern art in general, but a particular view of its purpose and development. Essentially, this consisted of establishing the belief that art was solely concerned with a self-referential reveling in artistic freedom, and the innovative fruits of the human spirit's inventive *élan*. Modern art, according to this view, had succeeded in sloughing off the dross of anecdote and sentimentalism, and the prosaic obligation of depicting the objective world. Within the Museum's framework, art became something asocial, apolitical, and collectable: suitable for exegesis by experts such as MOMA's curator, Alfred Barr. Photography's status as art had always been contested but MOMA, with the help of Adams, sought to give institutional weight to the idea that it could hold its own with painting and sculpture, even at their most modern. Adams' difference of opinion with Stieglitz concerning the role of MOMA may have been at root connected with Stieglitz's resentment at the upstaging of his privileged role as New York's, indeed, America's, residing impresario of modern art. Essentially they shared the same aims regarding the promotion of photography as a legitimate art form.

Adams' status as an official exponent of photography was reinforced in 1941 when he was appointed photo-muralist to the US Department of the Interior. In 1946 he founded the Department of Photography at the California School of Fine Arts. The same year his dedication to the Sierra was acknowledged by the award of a Guggenheim Fellowship in support of photographic studies of the national parks and monuments in America and Hawaii. This Fellowship was renewed in 1948. Adams' interest in technological innovation in the design and function of cameras was acknowledged by his appointment as consultant to the Polaroid Foundation in 1949.

Adams' virtuosity in handling his cameras, and in manipulating the negative in the printing process, has been widely acknowledged. To a degree that is almost paradoxically self-effacing, Adams always insisted on the primacy of technique in achieving suitably impeccable images. The resources of the medium, expanded whenever possible, provide the constraints within which the photographer tries to maximize pictorial intensity. In a series of articles under the general title 'On

Photography' written for *Camera Craft* between January and May 1934, Adams explained how he conceived of the role of technique.

In no other form of art is technique more closely interwoven than in photography. The photographer who thoroughly understands his medium visializes his subject as a thing-in-itself. He visualizes, therefore, before operating the shutter, the complete photograph. In order to do this he must be aware of every phase of technique. From the time of exposure to the mounting of the print . . . every link in the chain of production is vital in its contribution to the completed picture.

'Technique', he concluded, 'does not exist in itself, it is only the substance of the creative machinery.' Another manifestation of Adams' commitment to photographic education was his participation in the founding of the magazine *Aperture* in 1952 with Dorothea Lange, Minor White and Nancy and Beaumont Newhall.

Adams favored publishing his work in portfolios consisting of a small number of images. In this way he extended his scrupulous control over the nature of the image so as to define the framework in which the spectator would encounter it. His portfolios are equivalent to series of studies exemplifying technical variations on a grand theme, conceived of as part of a series, rather than as individual self-contained images. Together they offer a panorama of the land, from mountain tops to snow-covered tree branches. His energetic and arduous journeys across the Sierra produced relatively few images. This was partly because he was extremely exigent in his choice of motif, and partly because, once he returned to the dark room, he was equally uncompromising as to which images were worthy of printing. He was sanguine about the high expenditure of effort for quantitatively modest results: 'Twelve photographs that matter in a year is a good crop for any photographer.'

Ansel Adams died in 1984. His work has been widely published and collected. As yet, however, it has been venerated rather than studied as part of the elaboration of an American cultural identity. Nonetheless, whatever the historical significance of his work, Adams was an undeniably influential figure in American photography. His legacy has been twofold. By virtue of his perseverance with a limited range of subjects and an undeviating conception of his vocation, Adams effectively crystallized a certain vision of American landscape – mythic, empty, timeless, unique. During the 1960s, however, younger photographers reacted against what had become an inhibitingly one-dimensional 'straight photography' tradition, of which Adams was a prime exponent. In the work of Duane Michals and Diane Arbus, for example, the supposed directness of photography was subverted by focusing on the aberrant and disturbing.

Today, Adams' patriotic and pantheistic certainties have become untenable. It remains to be seen whether the resources of his photographic virtuosity can be harnessed to a new generation of ecological polemicism; whether the ubiquitous debris and environmental decay of the late twentieth century are as photogenic as the textures of undefiled nature which Adams strove so determinedly to capture.

Grand Teton
Grand Teton National Park,
Wyoming

10

12

Above

**Formations along the wall
of the Big Room, near the
Crystal Spring Home**
Carlsbad Caverns National Park,
New Mexico

Right

**Grand Canyon National
Park**
Grand Canyon National Park,
Arizona

14

Above
Canyon de Chelly
Canyon de Chelly, Arizona

Right
**The Giant Dome, largest
stalagmite thus far
discovered**
Carlsbad Caverns National Park,
New Mexico

16

Above
**Grand Canyon National
Park**
Panorama

Right
Yellowstone Falls
Yellowstone National Park,
Wyoming

18

Evening, McDonald Lake
Glacier National Park, Montana

19

20

In Glacier National Park
Glacier National Park, Montana

From Going-to-the-Sun Chalet
Glacier National Park, Montana

22

Heaven's Peak
Glacier National Park, Montana

Zion National Park
Zion National Park, Utah

24

Above
Center Peak, Center Basin
Kings River Canyon, California

Left
Saguaros
Saguaro National Monument,
Arizona

26

In Glacier National Park
Glacier National Park, Montana

**Jupiter Terrace – Fountain
Geyser Pool**

Yellowstone National Park,
Wyoming

Boulder Dam, 1941
Boulder Dam, Colorado

29

30

Church, Acoma Pueblo
Acoma Pueblo, New Mexico

31

In Glacier National Park
Glacier National Park, Montana

Above
Untitled
Mesa Verde National Park,
Colorado

Left
Canyon de Chelly
Canyon de Chelly, Arizona

Left
Church, Taos Pueblo
Taos Pueblo, New Mexico

Above
Church, Acoma Pueblo
Acoma Pueblo, New Mexico

36

Cliff Palace
Mesa Verde National Park,
Colorado

Mesa Verde National Park
Mesa Verde National Park,
Colorado

38

Right
At San Ildefonso Pueblo
San Ildefonso Pueblo, New
Mexico

Navajo Girl
Canyon de Chelly, Arizona

Left
Dance, San Ildefonso Pueblo
San Ildefonso Pueblo, New Mexico

41

Above
Navajo Woman and Child
Canyon de Chelly, Arizona

42

Above
Navajo Woman and Infant
Canyon de Chelly, Arizona

Right
**Dance, San Ildefonso
Pueblo**
San Ildefonso Pueblo, New
Mexico

ACKNOWLEDGMENTS

The publisher would like to thank Mike Rose,
who designed this book.
All photographs are courtesy the National Archives
with the exception of page 1: Bettmann Archive.